breeze-easy method 2

Clarinet

by Valentine Anzalone

over photo courtesy of the Selmer Company.

FOREWORD

This book, which has been written as a logical continuation of BREEZE-EASY BOOK I for CLARINET, thoroughly prepares the student for method books at the intermediate level. BREEZE-EASY BOOK II for CLARINET can also be used advantageously as a follow-up to any good beginning method. As with Book I, this book may be used with equally satisfying results either for private or for class work.

A playing knowledge of scales (major and chromatic) has been emphasized throughout the book in the belief that a mastery of scales is essential to the development of general technique and facility.

Special attention has been given to provide adequate review material in this book so that the student during the last lessons of the book is helped to retain the material he had previously learned.

Throughout the book you will find an abundance of melodic material which will serve to develop a cantabile style of playing in the student.

Valentine C. Anzalone

(All New Notes and Material will be placed in a box at the beginning of each lesson.)

LESSON 1.

SIXTEENTH NOTES

Moderato = At a medium tempo

1. Play the following scales from memory: C, F, G.

TEN LITTLE INDIANS

THEME FROM RAYMOND OVERTURE

THOMAS

THE MINSTREL BOY

Irish Folk Song

THIS LESSON HAS BEEN COMPLETED.   DATE.............................. EXCELLENT ☐ GOOD ☐ FAIR ☐

21503-28

LESSON 2.

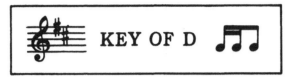

KEY OF D

THE D MAJOR SCALE

1.

THE C CHROMATIC SCALE

2.

3. a) $\downarrow$ 1 $\uparrow$ + $\uparrow$ 2 $\downarrow$ $\uparrow$ 1 da $\uparrow$ + $\downarrow$ 2 $\uparrow$ b)

4.

CZECH FOLK SONG (Duet)

Allegro

5. *f*

DANCE OF THE SPIRITS

GLUCK

Andante (Medium slow)

6. *mp*

THIS LESSON HAS BEEN COMPLETED.   DATE..............................   EXCELLENT ☐ GOOD ☐ FAIR ☐

LESSON 3.

1. Play the following scales from memory: C, F, G, D.

Four sixteenth notes equal one quarter note.

POLKA IN G

RHYTHM REVIEW

PRAIRIE SONG

Traditional

THIS LESSON HAS BEEN COMPLETED.   DATE.............................. EXCELLENT ☐ GOOD ☐ FAIR ☐

21503-28

6

LESSON 4.

1. Play the following scales from memory: C, F, G, D.

FARMER IN THE DELL

I'VE BEEN WORKING ON THE RAILROAD

RAPID SCALE STUDY

THIS LESSON HAS BEEN COMPLETED.   DATE............................ EXCELLENT ☐ GOOD ☐ FAIR ☐

LESSON 5.

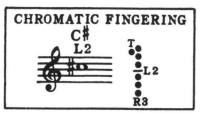

CHROMATIC FINGERING
C♯

THE B♭ MAJOR SCALE

MEMORIZE

1.

2. R2

3.

BATTLE HYMN OF THE REPUBLIC

Maestoso (Stately)   Traditional

4. mf

OH, MY DARLING CLEMENTINE

Traditional

5. mf

6. L1 R3 New ⊙ L2   L2 R3 L1

⊙ To play more smoothly and rapidly, the same little finger should not be used to play successive notes. Instead, alternate little fingers. In this book, the figures L1, L2, L3, R1, R2, or R3 above a note will indicate which little finger key to use. Refer to the FINGERING CHART on pages 30 and 31.

Upon completion of this lesson the student will find much enjoyment in playing from BREEZE-EASY PROGRAM PIECES-Book II by JOHN KINYON. This collection of well-known songs has been arranged in the simplest possible fashion and is available with piano accompaniment.

THIS LESSON HAS BEEN COMPLETED.   DATE.............................EXCELLENT ☐ GOOD ☐ FAIR ☐

LESSON 6.

REVIEW LESSON

1. Play the following scales from memory: C, F, G, D, B♭.

SIXTEENTH NOTE REVIEW ETUDE

LOW REGISTER REVIEW

OH! SUSANNA

FOSTER

THIS LESSON HAS BEEN COMPLETED.   DATE............................   EXCELLENT ☐ GOOD ☐ FAIR ☐

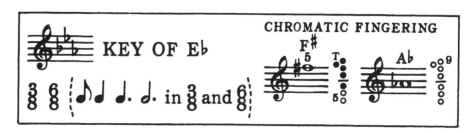

LESSON 7.

THE E♭ MAJOR SCALE

FAITH OF OUR FATHERS

DRINK TO ME ONLY WITH THINE EYES

Traditional

Key 5 is played with the third finger of the right hand.

THIS LESSON HAS BEEN COMPLETED.   DATE...................   EXCELLENT ☐ GOOD ☐ FAIR ☐

21503-28

LESSON 8.

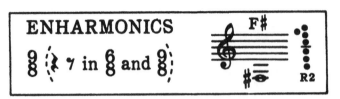

1. Play the following scales from memory: C, F, G, D, B♭, E♭.

ENHARMONIC TONES

BEAUTIFUL DREAMER

FOSTER

DE CAMPTOWN RACES

FOSTER

*Notes connected by arrows indicate enharmonic tones. These are tones which sound alike although written differently. The fingerings are the same.

THIS LESSON HAS BEEN COMPLETED.   DATE .... EXCELLENT ☐ GOOD ☐ FAIR ☐

LESSON 9.

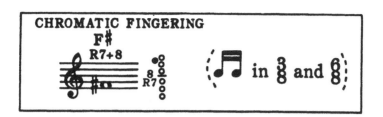

THE F CHROMATIC SCALE

MORNING
Allegretto — GRIEG

THE ASH GROVE
Moderato — Traditional

THIS LESSON HAS BEEN COMPLETED.   DATE .... EXCELLENT☐ GOOD☐ FAIR☐
21503-28

LESSON 10.

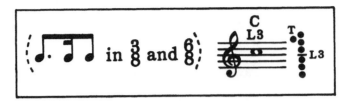

1. Play the following scales from memory: C, F, G, D, Bb, Eb, F Chromatic (see Lesson 9).

2.

These measures are played the same.

1 2 + 3   1 2 + 3   1 2 + 3

SONATA (Duet)

MOZART

Andante

3.

THE LEFT SIDE C

5.

Before or after Eb, always play C with the L3 Key.

SICILIAN MELODY

Moderato

6.

THIS LESSON HAS BEEN COMPLETED.   DATE .... EXCELLENT ☐ GOOD ☐ FAIR ☐

LESSON 11. |REVIEW LESSON|

1. Play the following scales from memory: C, F, G, D, B♭, E♭,
F Chromatic (see Lesson 9).

Use the **F♯** and **G♭** fingering requiring Key 5 only when indicated.

ETUDE IN D

HOME ON THE RANGE

Traditional

THIS LESSON HAS BEEN COMPLETED.   DATE .... EXCELLENT ☐ GOOD ☐ FAIR ☐

21503-28

14

LESSON 12.   REVIEW LESSON

1. Play the following scales from memory: C, F, G, B♭, E♭,
F Chromatic (Lesson 9).

GREENSLEEVES — English Folk Song

AN ENHARMONIC TEST

AMERICA THE BEAUTIFUL — WARD

THIS LESSON HAS BEEN COMPLETED.   DATE .... EXCELLENT ☐ GOOD ☐ FAIR ☐

21503-28

LESSON 13.

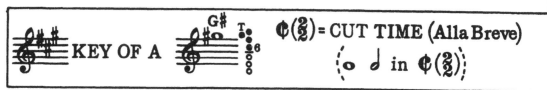

THE A MAJOR SCALE

ROUSSEAU'S HYMN

ALL THROUGH THE NIGHT

THIS LESSON HAS BEEN COMPLETED.   DATE ....   EXCELLENT ☐ GOOD ☐ FAIR ☐

21503-28

LESSON 14.

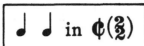

1. Play the following scales from memory: C, F, G, D, B♭, E♭, A,
F Chromatic (Lesson 9).

THE RALLY ROUSER (March)

V. C. A.

ETUDE IN D

Allegretto

THIS LESSON HAS BEEN COMPLETED.   DATE .... EXCELLENT☐ GOOD☐ FAIR☐

21503-28

LESSON 15.

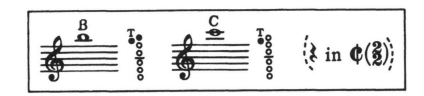

THE C MAJOR SCALE (Two Octaves)

THE F MAJOR SCALE (Two Octaves)

FINALE FROM ORPHEUS

OFFENBACH

Allegro

ETUDE IN E♭

Moderato

mf

THIS LESSON HAS BEEN COMPLETED.   DATE ....   EXCELLENT ☐ GOOD ☐ FAIR ☐

21503-28

LESSON 16.

1. Play the following scales from memory: C, F - - Two Octaves,
G, D, Bb, Eb, A - - One Octave.

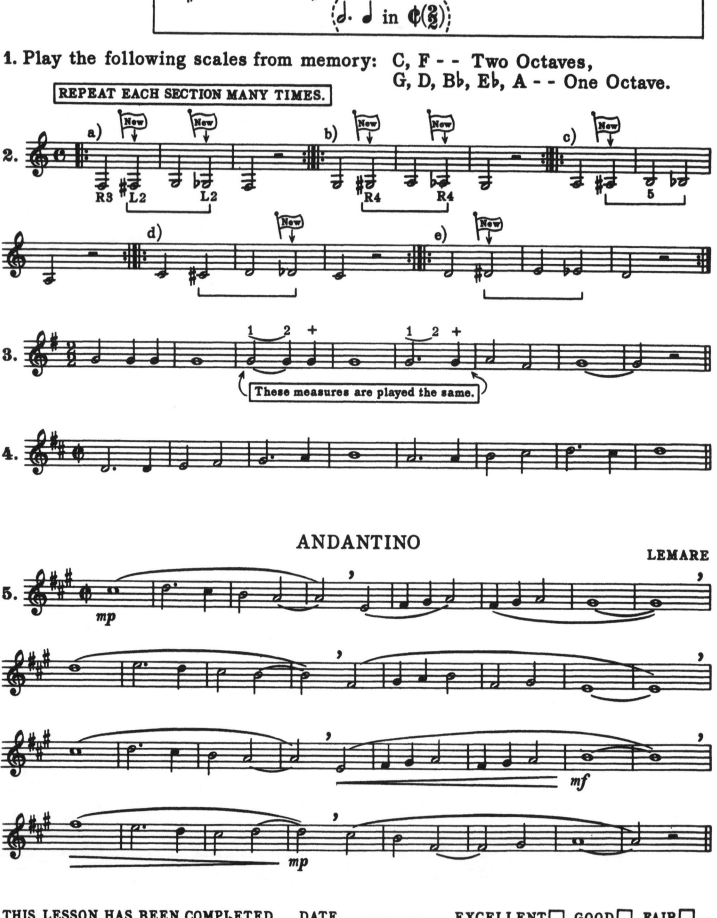

REPEAT EACH SECTION MANY TIMES.

These measures are played the same.

ANDANTINO

LEMARE

THIS LESSON HAS BEEN COMPLETED.   DATE.............................   EXCELLENT☐ GOOD☐ FAIR☐

21503-28

LESSON 17.

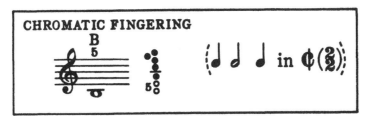

THE G MAJOR SCALE (Two Octaves)

1. MEMORIZE

CHROMATIC SCALE FROM LOW E

2. MEMORIZE

L1 R3 L2   5   5   L2 R3 L1

3. These measures are played the same.

4.

SALUTE TO THE TEAM (March)

V. C. A.

5. TRIO
   mf

MOMENT MUSICALE

SCHUBERT

6. Allegro
   mp

THIS LESSON HAS BEEN COMPLETED.   DATE ....   EXCELLENT ☐ GOOD ☐ FAIR ☐

21503-28

LESSON 18.

REVIEW LESSON

1. Play the following scales from memory: C, F, G -- Two Octaves,
D, B♭, E♭, A -- One Octave,
E Chromatic (Lesson 17).

REVIEW ETUDE #1

REVIEW ETUDE #2

BELIEVE ME IF ALL THOSE ENDEARING YOUNG CHARMS

Irish Air

THIS LESSON HAS BEEN COMPLETED.   DATE........................ EXCELLENT☐ GOOD☐ FAIR☐

21503-28

LESSON 19.

$\frac{6}{8}$ in 2

$\left(\text{♩.} \quad \text{♪.} \quad \text{in } \frac{6}{8} \text{(in 2)} \right)$

THE B♭ MAJOR SCALE (Two Octaves)

A $\frac{6}{8}$ MARCH

DOROTHY

SMITH

LOCH LOMOND

Old Scotch Air

At fast tempos it is more convenient to count only two beats in each $\frac{6}{8}$ measure.

THIS LESSON HAS BEEN COMPLETED.   DATE ....   EXCELLENT ☐ GOOD ☐ FAIR ☐

21503-28

LESSON 20.

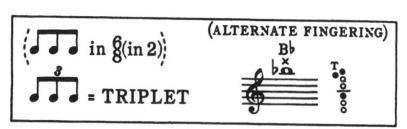

1. Play the following scales from memory: C, F, G, Bb - - Two Octaves,
D, A, Eb - - One Octave,
E Chromatic (Lesson 17).

Use the ✕ fingering when going to or from 5th line F

ANNIE LAURIE

SCOTT

⊛ Three equal notes to the beat are called a triplet.

THIS LESSON HAS BEEN COMPLETED.   DATE ....   EXCELLENT ☐   GOOD ☐   FAIR ☐

21503-28

LESSON 21.

♩ ♪ in ⁶⁄₈ (in 2) and ⁹⁄₈ (in 3)

THE A MAJOR SCALE (Two Octaves)

1. MEMORIZE

2. (in 2) — These measures are played the same.

POP! GOES THE WEASEL!

Traditional

3. Allegretto (in 2)

THREE BLIND MICE

Traditional Round

4. Allegretto (in 2)

5. (in 3) — mp

PILGRIMS' CHORUS

WAGNER

6. Maestoso — f — mf

THIS LESSON HAS BEEN COMPLETED. DATE............................. EXCELLENT ☐ GOOD ☐ FAIR ☐

21503-28

LESSON 22.

1. Play the following scales from memory: C, F, G, B♭, A -- Two Octaves, D, E♭ -- One Octave.

THE CHROMATIC SCALE

SPIRIT OF INDEPENDENCE

HOLZMANN

CHARLIE IS MY DARLING

Traditional

THIS LESSON HAS BEEN COMPLETED.   DATE............................   EXCELLENT☐   GOOD☐   FAIR☐

LESSON 23.

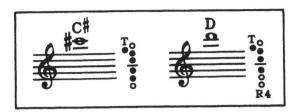

1. Play the following scales from memory: C, F, G, B♭, A -- Two Octaves,
E♭ -- One Octave,
Chromatic Scale (Lesson 22).

THE D MAJOR SCALE (Two Octaves)

VIVE L'AMOUR (Duet)

Traditional College Song

THIS LESSON HAS BEEN COMPLETED.   DATE............................   EXCELLENT ☐ GOOD ☐ FAIR ☐

21503-28

LESSON 24.

REVIEW LESSON

1. Play the following scales from memory: C, F, G, Bb, D, A -- Two Octaves,
Eb -- One Octave,
Chromatic Scale (Lesson 22).

2.

SUSY, LITTLE SUSY

3. Allegretto (in 3)

₵ REVIEW ETUDE

4. Moderato

JEANIE WITH THE LIGHT BROWN HAIR

FOSTER

5. Andante

THIS LESSON HAS BEEN COMPLETED.   DATE.............................   EXCELLENT☐   GOOD☐   FAIR☐

21503-28

LESSON 25. REVIEW LESSON

1. Play the following scales from memory: C, F, G, B♭, D, A -- Two Octaves,
E♭ -- One Octave,
Chromatic Scale (Lesson 22).

REVIEW ETUDE

THIS LESSON HAS BEEN COMPLETED.   DATE............................. EXCELLENT☐ GOOD☐ FAIR☐

21503-28

LESSON 26. □ REVIEW LESSON

1. Play the following scales from memory: C, F, G, B♭, D, A -- Two Octaves,
E♭ -- One Octave,
Chromatic Scale (Lesson 22).

BONNY DOON

Moderato (in 6)

Traditional

ETUDE IN D

THIS LESSON HAS BEEN COMPLETED.   DATE........................   EXCELLENT □   GOOD □   FAIR □

21503-28

LESSON 27. [REVIEW LESSON]

1. Play the following scales from memory: C, F, G, Bb, D, A -- Two Octaves,
Eb -- One Octave,
Chromatic Scale (Lesson 22).

CHROMATIC ETUDE

CZECH FOLK TUNE

THE CAMPBELLS ARE COMING

THIS LESSON HAS BEEN COMPLETED.   DATE............................   EXCELLENT☐   GOOD☐   FAIR☐

21503-28

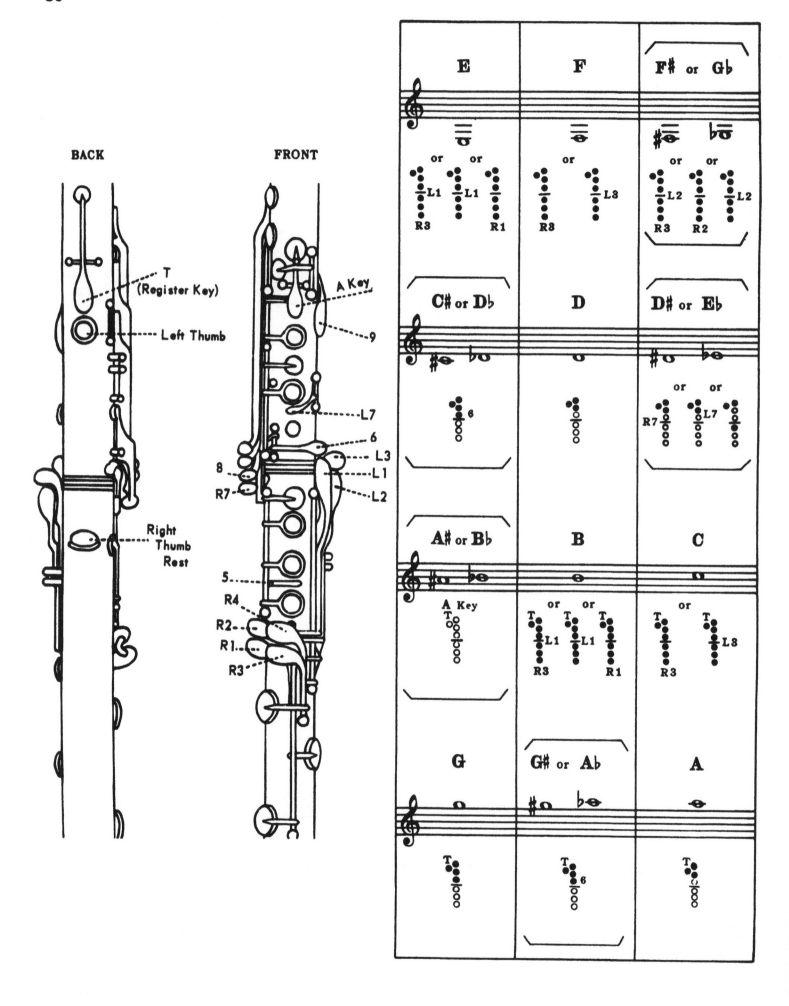

BACK

FRONT

FINGERING CHART

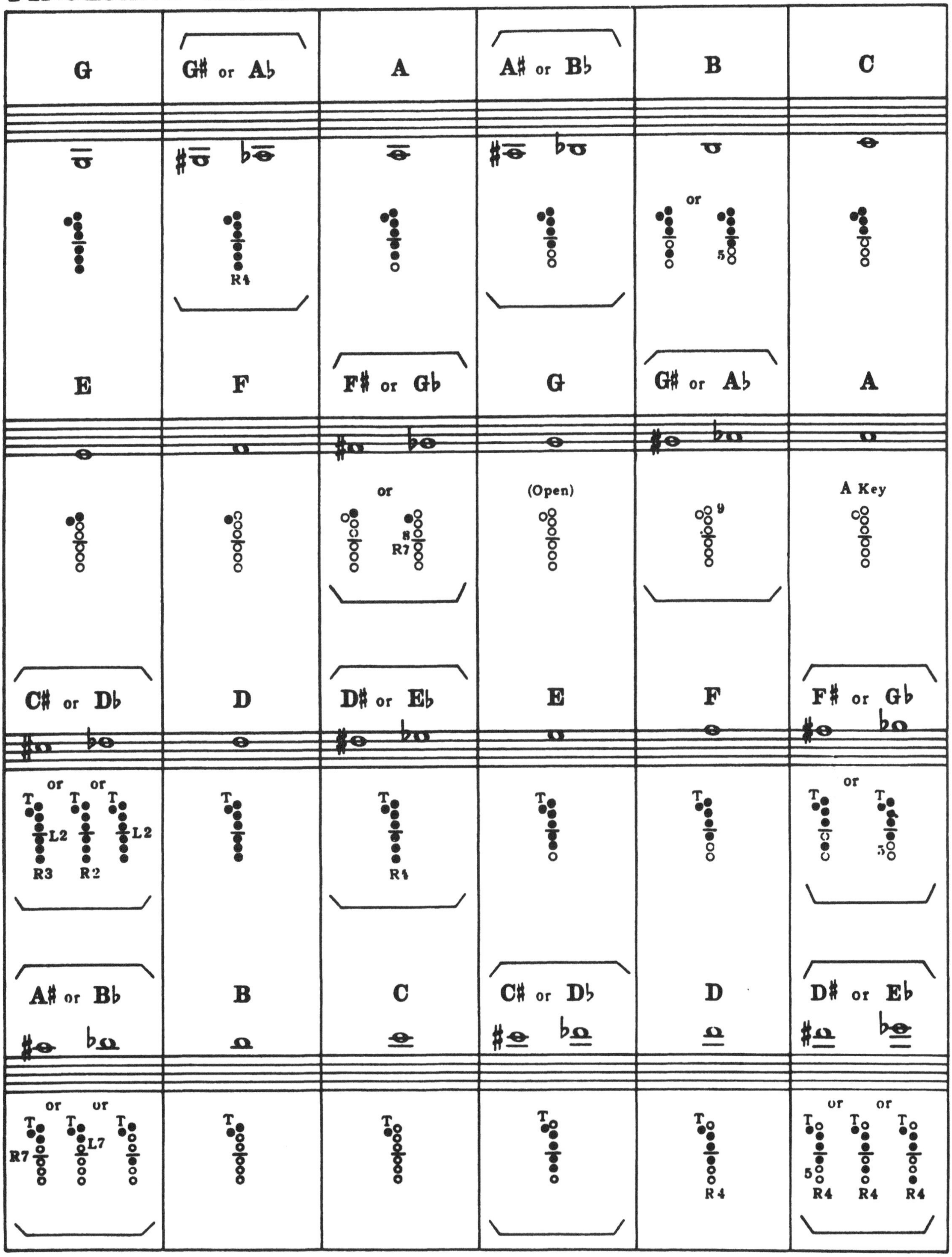

MAJOR⊛ SCALES (One Octave)

⊛ ALL MAJOR SCALES HAVE THE SAME PATTERN OF HALF AND WHOLE STEPS: